Danish History

500 Interesting Facts About Denmark

Welcome Aboard, Check Out This Limited-Time Free Bonus!

Ahoy, reader! Welcome to the Ahoy Publications family, and thanks for snagging a copy of this book! Since you've chosen to join us on this journey, we'd like to offer you something special.

Check out the link below for a FREE e-book filled with delightful facts about American History.

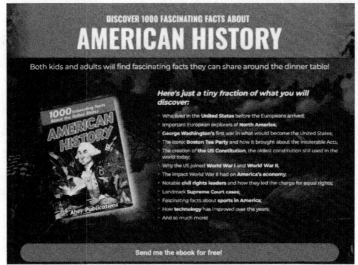

But that's not all - you'll also have access to our exclusive email list with even more free e-books and insider knowledge. Well, what are ye waiting for? Click the link below to join and set sail toward exciting adventures in American History.

Access your bonus here: https://ahoypublications.com/

Or, Scan the QR code!

Table of Contents

Introduction

The history of Denmark is a journey filled with rich cultural and political developments. From its early settlements thousands of years ago **to the Viking Age** conquests to **the Christianization of Denmark** to **the Reformation** and beyond, this small **Scandinavian country** has endured significant changes over many centuries.

In 1397, **the Kalmar Union was formed,** creating a unified Scandinavian state. This was followed by **the Great Northern War.** Struggling for Swedish power during the 1700s resulted in the unification of Schleswig, Holstein, and Lauenburg. By the time of WW, Denmark had become tired of devastating wars and accepted a policy of neutrality.

However, **the Nazi occupation of Denmark marked the dark ages** and brought about political and social changes, resulting in an economic rise along with the development of the welfare state.

In the 2000s, **Denmark witnessed rapid tourism growth,** followed by renewable energy initiatives and 21st-century digitalization and technology. **This book chronicles all these significant events** to provide readers with an insight into Denmark's history, culture, and development over the centuries.

Whether you are a history buff, a student, or simply curious about Denmark's past, **this book contains an array of information to help you explore one of Europe's oldest countries.** So, get ready to delve into **Denmark's captivating story!**

The Stone Age to the Bronze Age
(12,500 BCE– c. 500 CE)

This chapter **will explore the captivating prehistory of Denmark.** We'll take a look at **twenty interesting facts about life in this period,** from hunter-gatherers to the development of complex trade networks.

1. **The first evidence of people in Denmark dates to approximately 12,500 BCE.**

2. **The earliest people in Denmark were hunter-gatherers.** They gathered food from the land around them.

3. Between six thousand and ten thousand years ago, **Stone Age people began making tools and weapons** from flint stones found along coasts and rivers in Denmark.

4. **The Bronze Age started between 1800 and 1700 BCE.** People started using metal instead of stone or wood to make their tools and weapons.

5. In the 3rd millennium BCE, **the domesticated horse was introduced to Denmark.** Horses, along with the sun and ships, became a central element in Bronze Age religions.

6. **Horses were often buried with people,** showing they played a significant role in the spiritual beliefs of the early Danish people.

7. From 3000 to 800 BCE, **people lived in small villages.** They lived in roundhouses made out of wood or stone.

8. **Ironworking began in Denmark and the rest of Scandinavia** around 500 BCE. Danes gained access to stronger materials for building weapons, farm implements, and jewelry.

9. Around 1000 BCE, **people in Denmark started trading with other nearby regions,** exchanging goods like pottery, clay figurines, and ornaments.

10. **One of the more famous finds from the Bronze Age period in Denmark is the Trundholm sun chariot,** a bronze sculpture just under two feet long. The Trundholm sun chariot consists of a bronze figure of a horse pulling a disk-shaped sun chariot.

11. **The sun disk is made of a thin sheet of gold and is highly decorated with intricate details.** The horse, chariot, and sun disk are all mounted on wheels, allowing it to be rolled. It is well preserved and gives us a glimpse into the religious beliefs of the time.

12. Archaeological finds in Denmark and the surrounding area indicate that **during the Late Bronze Age, people crafted boats** that could hold about a dozen people. These boats bore a resemblance to the later, more **famous Viking ships, though the earlier boats had no sails.**

13. **During the Early Iron Age, many different groups of people lived in or had contact with the area of Denmark and northern Germany,** including Germanic people, Celts, Slavs, and others.

14. By 500 BCE, **the people of Denmark traded across the North Sea** into present-day Norway and Sweden, as well as south into present-day Germany and east into the Baltic region.

15. It's believed that between 800 and 500 BCE, the religious beliefs of the area, including parts of Germany, **began to worship the gods that later became famous during the Viking Age, such as Thor and Odin.**

16. **The Late Iron Age in northern Europe (400– 800 CE) comprises the Migration Period, the Merovingian Period** (the name of the dominant Frankish tribe in the region), and **the early Viking Age.**

17. **The Migration Period** (375–568 CE) **was marked by migrations and interactions among Germanic tribes, including the Danes.**

18. **The Borum Eshøj burial mound, dating from the Early Iron Age** (around 700 BCE), **is one of Denmark's largest and most significant burial sites.** It contains a chamber **tomb with a rich assortment of grave goods, including pottery, metal objects, and personal items.** The mound provides valuable information about the social and religious aspects of the Iron Age.

19. One of **the reasons there have been so many well-preserved bodies and other finds in Denmark is because many were located in bogs.** Scandinavian bogs are cold and relatively current-free, allowing animal, human, and wooden remains to stay relatively well preserved. **One of the most famous bog bodies found in Denmark is the Tollund Man, dating back to around 375 to 210 BCE.**

20. **Runestones were erected during this period in Denmark** as a way to remember the dead or mark important events.

Viking Age
(793–1050)

Explore the rich and impressive history of the Viking Age. In this chapter, we will take a look at **twenty interesting facts about those famous warriors** who raided and journeyed throughout much of the known world and beyond.

21. By 793, **Scandinavians from Denmark, Norway, and Sweden began to raid other lands in Europe** and beyond. This era is now known as the Viking Age.

22. **The Vikings were skilled sailors who used their longboats to travel across oceans and rivers far from home.**

23. **In 865, Viking raids began to spread across Europe as more and more warriors joined their ranks from different parts of Scandinavia,** including Sweden and Norway.

24. **Viking raiders became feared across Europe due to their raids on monasteries** filled with religious artifacts for plunder.

25. **Vikings weren't just raiders and warriors. They were traders. During this time,** Viking trade began to expand to include most of Europe, as well as parts of the Middle East.

26. **Goods from as far away as China have been discovered in archaeological sites dating from the Viking period.** Silver coins from the Arabian Peninsula were highly prized and widely used at this time.

27. **One of the first powerful Viking kings was Horik I in the early 9th century,** but it wasn't until one hundred years or so later that **King Gorm "the Old" and his son, Harald Bluetooth, united the country under their rule.**

28. **Harald Bluetooth is indeed the namesake of the famous "Bluetooth" technology you use every day.**

29. **The Jelling stones were carved by order of King Harald Bluetooth around 965.** Most of the runestones in Denmark and elsewhere in Scandinavia have **Christian references or symbols, indicating the spread of the religion in the later part of the Viking Age.**

30. **The Danes and other Scandinavians developed a unique and early form of representative government called a "thing,"** in which people could raise issues and grievances.

31. **The Vikings explored and conquered lands in England and Ireland and settled Iceland and Greenland.**

32. **After the death of Harald Bluetooth in 986, King Sweyn Forkbeard became king**. His son Canute, sometimes called **Canute the Great,** took it a step further. Through conquest, diplomacy, and marriage, he became **king of Denmark, Norway, and England.**

33. **The Danes ruled much of northern and central England between 1016 and 1042.** This area was called **the Danelaw** because Danish law was dominant there.

34. **The Vikings used the city of York as their capital in England,** though they called it Jorvik.

35. **Skilled artisans all over Denmark and Scandinavia created beautiful and intricate metalwork,** such as brooches, jewelry, coins, and other decorations for wealthy individuals.

36. **Much of what we know about the Danish Vikings comes from later accounts written in Scandinavia** and accounts of more literate foreigners, like the English.

37. **Although the English accounts are a great source of information, they are also biased against the Vikings for many reasons,** including religion.

38. **The Vikings were not a very literate people**. Like many cultures in history, they mostly spread history and events by word of mouth.

39. Though there were always exceptions, **Danish and Norwegian Vikings usually headed west, while Swedish Vikings developed trade and kingdoms in modern-day Russia and Ukraine.**

40. **Ragnar Lothbrok, the Viking "king" made famous in the TV series Vikings,** may or may not have existed. In the series, **he and his people are from the town of Kattegat,** which is not the actual name of a town but rather a body of water that connects the North and Baltic Seas around Denmark.

Christianization of Denmark
(950s–1100s)

This chapter will explore the fascinating history of Christianity in Denmark. Let's take a look at **twenty interesting facts about how Christianity** spread throughout the region. Do you think people embraced the religion?

41. **Denmark was originally a pagan country,** but in the 950s, it began to convert to Christianity.

42. In 965, **King Harald Bluetooth, the king who unified Denmark, converted to Christianity.** Some historians believe that Harald converted because he truly believed in God, while others believe he converted for trade advantages.

43. **The people of Denmark were slow to accept this new faith. Many held on to their Viking beliefs for years.**

44. **During Harald's reign, churches and monasteries were built throughout the nation,** spreading Christian ideas throughout his kingdom.

45. **Canute the Great's rule helped spread Christian beliefs among the Danes, but the Norwegians were more resistant to the Christian faith.** It wasn't until the 1100s that Norway became a largely Christian country.

46. **Following the death of Canute the Great in 1035, Danish kings continued to support and encourage the spread of Christian beliefs in their lands.**

47. **The first Dane made a saint** (called "canonization") by **the Catholic Church was King Canute IV** (c. 1043–1086). **He strongly supported Christianity in Denmark.** Canute was killed inside a church in 1086 by rebellious nobles led by his brother, who became **King Olaf I.**

48. **During King Valdemar I's reign** (r. 1154–1182), **the first Danish bishopric was established in Lund.** This helped bring more priests from other parts of Europe into Denmark who could help spread Christian teachings.

49. **The first cathedral in Denmark was the Ribe Cathedral, located in Ribe, Denmark.** It was constructed during the 12th and 13th centuries.

50. From 1210 to 1220, **Archbishop Eskil began introducing new laws and regulations on how Christians should behave and live their lives while also restricting old pagan beliefs among his people.**

51. **The Catholic Church slowly began to build schools throughout Denmark.** As a result, the literacy rate in Denmark began to improve, especially among the upper classes, many of whom learned Latin, the language of the Catholic Church.

52. **Children were taught Christian values in primary schools.** Universities provided more advanced instruction on topics like religion and philosophy.

53. Though there had been settlements and buildings in the area for centuries, **Copenhagen, the capital of Denmark, began to thrive in the late 12th and early 13th centuries.** One church leader, **Bishop Absalon of Lund,** is credited with increasing the size and wealth of Copenhagen in the late 1100s.

54. In the 1300s, **Danish churches started to become more decorative with paintings and sculptures of Christian figures** so that people could better relate the church's teachings to their everyday lives.

55. **Church services and the Bible were always in Latin,** which was, for the most part, not understood by the Danish people.

56. **By the 1400s, a majority of Danes had converted fully to Christianity, although many kept some pagan traditions alive.** For example, many old traditions, such as the decorated tree and the Yule log, were incorporated into the Christian holiday of Christmas.

57. By the 1400s, **the church had imposed strict laws on citizens, including bans against adultery or any kind** of physical relationship outside marriage.

58. As part of the Christianization process, **many pagan places of worship were destroyed or converted into churches.**

59. **Witchcraft was heavily persecuted during this era by clergymen. Punishments ranged anywhere from public humiliation to the death penalty,** depending on the severity of the offense committed.

60. **Elements of old pagan beliefs, like the belief in elves and trolls, are still around today,** although they are nowhere near as prominent as they once were.

The Black Death and the Kalmar Union
(c. 1348–1523)

Discover the history of the Kalmar Union and its impact on Scandinavia in this chapter. We'll explore **twenty facts about this union,** as well as the dreaded Black Death.

61. In 1348, **an outbreak known as the Black Death spread throughout Europe from East Asia,** causing a plague that killed millions, including thousands in Denmark alone

62. **The Black Death caused many disruptions to daily life, such as food shortages that led some Danes away from the farmlands and into cities,** causing the disease to spread and grow faster in crowded conditions.

63. **The Black Death caused a temporary decline in the Danish population from about 500,000 people to 300,000.** The population eventually recovered by 1523 when **the Kalmar Union** ended.

64. **After the plague had passed, there was an increase in immigration into Denmark,** largely due to the work opportunities created by rebuilding efforts across Europe.

65. **The widespread deaths of the Black Death impacted the economies of Scandinavia.** The wars they often fought between them were also costly in terms of money and lives.

66. **The Kalmar Union was a union between Denmark, Norway, and Sweden in 1397.**

67. During this period, **kings from each country ruled over their respective countries but had to abide by common laws set out in the union agreement.**

68. **Queen Margrethe I** (1353–1412) **of Denmark formed the union to keep peace among the three nations.** She created a united kingdom under her rule.

69. **Margrethe I is considered by many historians to be one of the most powerful women in European history,** but she often gets overlooked. **The present queen of Denmark** and the longest serving European monarch alive as of 2023, took the name Margrethe as her royal name when she was crowned in 1972.

70. During this period, **the Danish people relied heavily on trade for their economic survival, primarily trading with Germany and other parts of Europe.**

71. **Margarethe I was born in Søborg Castle, located just across the straits from today's Sweden.** Today, it is in ruins, but it had served as a castle and prison.

72. During this time, **Danish merchants were involved in trading with countries like Portugal and England,** which helped to improve the Danish people's quality of life and the economy.

73. **Though direct trade between Asia and Denmark didn't really flourish until the Age of Discovery,** it was not unheard of for Asian goods like teak and ivory to be found.

74. **The Kalmar Union also included the Danish possessions of Iceland and Greenland,** though their distance meant they were governed by local nobles or governors appointed by **the Danish king.**

75. **The Kalmar Union marked a time when Denmark became more involved with international politics,** forming alliances and becoming part of the global trade network.

76. **Political, dynastic, religious, and ethnic tensions eventually caused the union to begin to unravel** in the early part of the 1500s.

77. By 1517, **Lutheranism had begun gaining traction within Scandinavia, leading some people away from Catholicism toward Protestantism** and causing further religious tension between members of the union.

78. **Though it was one of the first attempts in history to form a multinational union, the Kalmar Union eventually failed.** The prime reason behind its failure was the Swedish War of Independence, in which Sweden fought to eliminate Danish possession of the southern part of their country.

79. **The union was also weakened by the lack of uniform policies, including taxation.**

80. **Norway remained part of the Danish kingdom from the 14th century until 1814,** when it became, at least officially, part of Sweden via a treaty.

The Reformation Years in Denmark
(1536–1660)

Explore Denmark's Reformation period in this chapter. During this transformative era, **Lutheranism became the official religion, leading to significant changes in education, churches, and daily life.** Let's explore some facts about this pivotal moment in Danish history!

81. In 1536, **King Christian III of Denmark signed the Lutheran Church Ordinance,** which made Lutheranism the official religion of Denmark.

82. The Reformation period lasted from 1536 to around 1660. **It was a time when religious beliefs changed in much of northern Europe,** with people converting from Catholicism to Protestantism.

83. During this time, **Danish churches were stripped of Catholic symbols like statues of saints** that had been used for many centuries.

84. Like most of the nations of northern and central Europe, **Denmark was involved in the costly Thirty Years' War, which was largely fought between Catholics and Protestants.**

85. **Though Denmark retained its Protestant beliefs, the war was costly to Denmark** in terms of land lost, the economy, prestige, and, of course, the thousands of people killed.

86. **The Bible was translated into Danish during this period so people could read it themselves** instead of trusting what priests told them about its teachings or having access only through Latin translations available at certain monasteries or universities.

87. In 1550, **King Christian III issued an edict requiring everyone to attend church services and take communion at least once a year.**

88. The first printed hymnal in Danish was published in 1569, allowing churches to sing newly composed Lutheran songs as part of their worship service.

89. In 1551, **Christian III issued an edict that all marriages must be performed by ministers of the Lutheran Church** or else they were not legally binding.

90. In 1559, **there was a nationwide reform of the school curriculum, which included subjects such as geography, history, mathematics, and the natural sciences.** Many of these classes were held in Danish rather than Latin. This allowed a broader segment of the population to get an education.

91. For a time, **the new Lutheran authorities in Denmark became even more intrusive than the Catholic Church** had been, governing or stressing the importance of dress and public and private behavior.

92. **Christian IV** (r. 1588–1648) **issued laws and guidelines instructing architects and builders to construct churches in a safe manner using quality materials.** He also issued guidelines for design, which increased the appeal of the buildings.

93. **During the Reformation, parish records became mandatory throughout Denmark,** so births, deaths, and other important events could be tracked accurately within each district.

94. **It wasn't until the 19th century that laws stressing religious equality were passed, giving Danish Catholics and Jews equal rights** and the right to hold public worship without government and societal harassment or interference.

95. One **important figure from this time was the theologian Niels Hemmingsen,** who wrote several books about Lutheranism and its teachings.

96. **Though the Reformation began as a struggle against the Catholic Church,** there were serious arguments and even violence between the various Protestant sects throughout Europe.

97. **The Evangelical Lutheran Church of Denmark became the state-sponsored church of the country in 1849.**

98. After the Reformation in 1536, many **Catholics fled Denmark, as Lutheranism became the state religion.** Catholic practices were suppressed.

99. **Today, Catholics make up a small minority in Denmark,** making up approximately 1 to 2 percent of the population. **The majority of Danes belong to the Evangelical Lutheran Church,** the state church of Denmark, though most Danes are non-practicing.

100. **The leading figure of the Danish Reformation was Hans Tausen** (1494–1561), known as the **"Martin Luther of Denmark."** He spread Lutheran ideas and translated and preached doctrines that influenced the establishment of Lutheranism as the state religion.

The Northern Seven Years' War
(1563–1570)

Explore the intriguing Northern Seven Years' War, a conflict that unfolded in Denmark between 1563 and 1570. In this chapter, we'll delve into **twenty captivating facts about the war's origins, battles, and consequences for the Danish.**

101. **The Northern Seven Years' War was a conflict that saw Denmark and Norway pitted against Sweden** from 1563 to 1570.

102. There were many causes of the **Northern Seven Years' War, from territorial disputes to questions about trade and influence in the Baltic region** around Denmark and Sweden.

103. The major cause of **the Northern Seven Years' War,** at least as far as Denmark was concerned, was **Denmark's rivalry with Sweden over control of trade routes and territorial disputes in the Baltic region.**

104. **King Frederick II of Denmark sought to maintain Danish dominance over the Baltic Sea and secure control of lucrative trade routes,** which were being increasingly threatened by Sweden's growing power under **King Eric XIV.**

105. **The Swedes attacked the remaining Danish forts in what is now Sweden and engaged in naval battles with the Danish/Norwegian navy at sea.**

106. **There were periods of peace during the Northern Seven Years' War.** One notable truce was **the Treaty of Roskilde, signed in 1568,** which temporarily halted hostilities between Denmark-Norway and Sweden. However, fighting resumed shortly after, and the war continued until the final peace settlement.

107. **Sweden violated a truce agreement with an assault on Varberg Fortress** in 1564. Denmark retook the fortress in 1569.

108. **The vast majority of the battles of the war were fought in today's Sweden.**

109. In 1567, **the Danish Navy prepared for a full-scale attack on Swedish coasts** and succeeded in taking control of several islands before peace negotiations began in June 1568.

110. **Denmark and Sweden signed an armistice treaty at Stettin,** located in modern-day Poland, in September 1570, which ended all military actions between them until 1645.

111. **The Northern Seven Years' War resulted in many towns being destroyed** or taken by enemy forces. Many lives were lost as well.

112. **Resources were prevented from reaching Denmark due to Swedish blockades** at sea in the north and land in the south.

113. **King Frederick II renounced all claims to Sweden under the Treaty of Stettin. The Swedish king recognized Halland, Blekinge, and parts of Skane** (all of which were in Sweden) as belonging to Denmark.

114. **The Northern Seven Years' War is seen as a turning point in Danish history.** It marked the beginning of the decline of Danish military power and the rise of Sweden.

115. **The most famous Danish military leader during the war was Admiral Herluf Trolle,** who engaged in a number of naval battles against the Swedes. He died from wounds received in battle in June 1565.

116. **Denmark faced many challenges during the war. Their navy was smaller and less experienced.** Sweden had powerful allies that aided it economically, and its forces were better led on land.

117. Despite all these setbacks, many historians agree that **the Northern Seven Years' War helped strengthen Danish national identity and patriotism among its citizens.**

118. After 1570, **both sides agreed upon set boundaries between them that lasted until 1645 when the Torstenson War broke out** over disputed territories in what is now modern-day Germany and Poland.

119. **Frederick II of Denmark was initially quite popular, especially because he was seen as a strong defender of Denmark's territory.** However, the cost of the war and the territorial losses the country sustained during the conflict cost Frederick II much goodwill in his realm.

120. **The Northern Seven Years' War shaped Denmark's** approach to diplomacy and the territorial disputes that popped up in the years that followed.

Danish Colonies and Trade Monopoly Abroad
(1600s–1700s)

This chapter will explore the far-reaching **impact of Danish colonization and trade.** We'll take a look at **twenty facts about Denmark's trading networks,** colonies, and involvement in the Atlantic slave trade.

121. **Denmark's first overseas colony was Tranquebar in India.** Tranquebar was founded in 1620.

122. Although Danes had visited, settled, and traded in Greenland for some time, it wasn't until the 1700s **that Greenland officially became a possession of the Danish Crown.**

123. **The Danes relied on traditional trading routes to transport goods from their colonies back to Europe.** They imported sugarcane, tobacco, spices, timber, and animal hides.

124. In 1670, **King Christian V granted the Danish East India Company exclusive rights over all trade with Asia,** which gave it a monopoly for more than one hundred years.

125. **For much of this period, the Danes developed commercial networks throughout Africa and Asia,** making them one of the world's largest trading and economic powers at that time.

126. **The Danes were established in many European trading posts** in cities like Amsterdam and Antwerp to support their lucrative overseas operations.

127. **They also maintained trading stations in many ports in West African slave-trading regions like Fort Christiansborg and Elmina Castle in Ghana.**

128. During the 1700s, **Danish traders were heavily involved in the Atlantic slave trade,** buying and selling enslaved Africans as part of their lucrative business ventures.

129. **Denmark had a monopoly on trade with Greenland,** which ensured they benefited from its resources, such as fish oil, seal hides, and whale blubber.

130. **The American Virgin Islands once belonged to Denmark.** Twice during the Napoleonic era, Great Britain seized the islands from Denmark without a shot being fired.

131. **When the Napoleonic Wars ended in 1815, the modern-day US Virgin Islands were returned to Denmark,** which was never able to profit from them.

132. **Denmark experienced a difficult economic time during WWI and sold the Virgin Islands to the US in 1917.**

133. At various times through the 19th century, **Denmark controlled the Virgin Islands** (known then as the Danish West Indies), **Greenland, the Faroe Islands, Iceland, parts of Ghana and other trading posts in West Africa,** trading posts on the coast of present-day Sri Lanka and on India's southeastern coast.

134. **By the 1800s, Denmark had become a lesser economic power than it had been in previous centuries.** It was competing less successfully with Britain, France, and Holland for overseas trade.

135. **Though Iceland was a Danish possession, during the 1800s,** the Icelanders gained more and more autonomy. **In 1944, Icelanders declared independence from Denmark,** which was occupied by Nazi Germany at the time.

136. By the late 1800s, **Danish colonies outside of Europe had been sold off or abandoned.** All that remained were Greenland (which is now an autonomous country within the Kingdom of Denmark), Iceland, the Faroe Islands, and the Danish West Indies (until 1917).

137. **The most prosperous Danish colony was Saint Thomas, though the Danish Crown still lost money with this venture.** Saint Thomas has a deep port and, for a time, was the leading producer of rum in the world. It also produced a lot of sugar.

138. It's important to remember that **Danish businesses relied on slave labor to make money for much of their history in the West Indies.** Denmark abolished the slave trade in 1792, although the decree didn't go into effect until 1803. In 1848, slavery was abolished.

139. **Despite being a small nation with limited resources and military power,** Denmark was able to maintain control over its overseas territories through shrewd negotiations and diplomatic skills.

140. **The most famous Danish explorer of the time was Vitus Bering, after whom the Bering Straits between Russia and the USA were named.** He made voyages to the west coast of northern North America and the far east of present-day Russia.

Great Northern War
(1700–1721)

Discover the remarkable story of the Great Northern War and its impact on Denmark and Norway. Throughout their united history, **Denmark was the dominant partner in the union with Norway.** It offered protection to less populated Norway, but it also dominated Norway's foreign affairs. This chapter will explore twenty interesting facts about this pivotal conflict.

141. **In 1700, the Great Northern War began between the Swedish Empire and a coalition of countries,** including the Tsardom of Russia, Denmark-Norway, and Saxony-Poland (later Poland-Lithuania).

142. **Charles XII of Sweden aimed to gain control over territories from Denmark, asserting Swedish dominance in the Baltic.** He sought to prevent Danish alliances with Russia and Poland-Lithuania. He also wanted to enhance Sweden's economic and trade control.

143. **Charles XII's personal ambition to restore Sweden's power and achieve glory were a major factor behind his decision to embark upon the Great Northern War.**

144. Denmark-Norway's initial involvement in **the Great Northern War began with an invasion of the Swedish-held territories in the Duchy of Holstein-Gottorp** in February 1700.

145. In late July 1700, **Charles XII of Sweden launched a swift amphibious assault on Zealand, landing near Humlebæk and advancing toward Copenhagen.**

146. **The landing at Humlebæk and the rapid advance toward Copenhagen highlighted Sweden's military capabilities** and set the stage for subsequent phases of the war.

147. **The attack on Zealand pressured Denmark-Norway into signing the Treaty of Travendal** on August 18th, 1700, temporarily ending hostilities.

148. **Denmark-Norway rejoined the war in 1709 as part of an anti-Swedish coalition,** aiming to regain lost territories and weaken Sweden's position in the Baltic region.

149. Today, **Copenhagen is the capital of one of the most peaceful countries on Earth,** but during the first part of **the Great Northern War** and later in **the Napoleonic period**, the city was the scene of battles and destructive naval bombardments.

150. One of **the significant battles involving Denmark was the Battle of Helsingborg in 1710.** Danish forces attempted to recapture Scania but were ultimately defeated by the Swedish army, forcing them to retreat.

151. **The Peace of Frederiksborg in 1720 solidified Danish gains, ending the war with Sweden.**

152. **The damage inflicted on both sides had been tremendous.** It would take decades before they fully recovered.

153. **Denmark-Norway also received monetary compensation from Sweden as part of the Treaty of Frederiksborg,** helping to offset the costs of the war.

154. **The Great Northern War marked a change in national policies in both Denmark and Sweden.** As a result of the war, both kingdoms began to concentrate less on overseas events and more on domestic affairs.

155. **Following the Great Northern War, the Danes adopted a policy of neutrality toward their neighbors,** which helped them maintain peace for many years until the Napoleonic Wars began for Denmark in the early years of the 19th century.

156. **Swedish King Charles XII, the last of the Swedish "warrior kings," was killed during the siege of Fredriksten in Norway in 1718.**

157. As a result of **the Danish defeat at Copenhagen, the city's fortifications were rebuilt and improved.** These would later serve as major defenses during **the Napoleonic Wars.**

158. Today, **Frederick IV's image in Denmark is complex.** He is remembered for his patronage of the arts and focus on domestic improvements, and he is credited with boosting Danish culture.

159. **Frederick IV's failure to abolish serfdom and the economic strain of the Great Northern War cast a shadow,** though. Though not universally popular, he's likely seen as a well-meaning but ultimately not wholly successful monarch.

160. **After the Great Northern War, Denmark engaged in only one more war on its territory until its very short involvement in WWII.** That conflict was the War of 1864 against Prussia and Austria, which it lost.

Reform Period of Johann Struensee
(1770–1772)

We'll uncover twenty interesting facts about this pivotal period in history, which saw **King Christian VII's physician, Johann Struensee, usher in progressive reforms to benefit all citizens equally.**

161. In the late 1700s, **Denmark was ruled by King Christian VII.**

162. In 1768, a **German-Danish doctor and philosopher named Johann Struensee became the king's physician and close advisor.**

163. **Struensee used his position to lead a period of reform in Denmark.** Historians consider this part of the Age of Enlightenment.

164. **The Age of Enlightenment was part of the immensely important Age of Reason when scientific and intellectual discoveries** led to the beginning of the "modern world" as we know it.

165. **Enlightenment thinkers and lawmakers were largely focused on the rights of the individual** and improvements that could be made in the lives of the average person, not just royals and nobles.

166. **Struensee passed laws that abolished torture for criminals and made education compulsory for all children between six and twelve years old,** even those from poorer families.

167. **Struensee introduced freedom of religion and free speech in public places such as churches, town halls, and theaters.** This meant it wasn't illegal to express one's opinion.

168. Because of these changes, Denmark achieved a higher level of literacy during this time.

169. **While Struensee implemented various reforms aimed at modernizing Denmark and improving the welfare of its citizens,** the Danish government remained an absolute monarchy.

170. **Although some very positive changes occurred because of Struensee's reforms,** they weren't without opposition. Traditionalists criticized the new direction Denmark was heading in and wanted to limit Struensee's powers.

171. **Struensee had an affair with Queen Caroline Matilda, which resulted in a child, Princess Louise Augusta.** The affair and Struensee's increasing power resulted in a coup in 1772.

172. **Struensee and the queen were arrested.** She was sent into exile, but Struensee was killed.

173. **The princess was proclaimed the king's daughter,** but everyone knew she was the daughter of Struensee.

174. **This period saw an increase in trade with other countries, meaning Denmark's economy flourished** while prices dropped on everyday items like sugar and coffee beans, making them accessible for many households.

175. **During the late 18th and early 19th centuries, Denmark spent considerable amounts of money on modern infrastructure and agricultural reforms.** The Danes built roads and bridges, planted trees, and introduced new crop rotation techniques.

176. **After Johann Struensee was overthrown, the power in Denmark was once again concentrated in the hands of King Christian VII,** although the king's ability to govern effectively remained limited due to his mental health issues.

177. **The Danish nobility and the Privy Council played significant roles in the administration of the country.**

178. **Despite Struensee's removal from power and execution,** many of his reforms exist today, such as compulsory education for all children between six and twelve years old.

179. **The year 1848 saw a new Danish king, Frederick VII,** who was more reform-minded and able than his father. He introduced many reforms, such as ending the absolute monarchy in Denmark.

180. In 1849, **Frederick put forward the Constitution of 1849, which included most if not all of the reforms you just read about.** Even though there have been new constitutions written since the Constitution of 1849, it serves as the groundwork for Danish civil and political society today.

Denmark and the Napoleonic Wars
(early 1800s)

Explore the engaging history of one of Europe's most decisive conflicts in this chapter as we **uncover twenty interesting facts about Denmark's role in the Napoleonic Wars** and the nation's fate after **the Battle of Copenhagen.**

181. In the late 1700s, **Denmark was part of an alliance against France called the Second Coalition.**

182. **The Second Coalition fought against the revolutionary forces of France,** which had begun its revolution in 1789, overthrown its king in 1792, and were spreading anti-monarchical ideas throughout Europe.

183. **Napoleon Bonaparte rose to power in France in 1799** and continued France's war with Britain and its allies.

184. **During the Napoleonic Wars, Britain enforced a naval embargo on France,** which prevented other countries from trading with France. **At the time, Britain had the most powerful navy in the world** and could easily enforce the embargo.

185. **Some of the countries affected by the embargo believed it was an attack on their freedom of trade and entertained the thought of joining Napoleon.** One of them was the Union of Denmark and Norway, which had a powerful navy at the time.

186. **To prevent the Danish/Norwegian navy from being used against British ships, the British attacked the Danish/Norwegian fleet in Copenhagen.**

187. **The British attack was led by the famous British Admiral Horatio Nelson.** It took place on April 2nd, 1801. It is known as the First Battle of Copenhagen.

188. **Denmark was forced to sign a peace treaty with Britain and reestablish normal diplomatic relations with the British.** It also forced Denmark to break relations with France.

189. By 1807, **Denmark had built a sizable fleet. Although Denmark was a neutral country,** the British were still afraid that the Danish/Norwegian fleet would fall into Napoleon Bonaparte's hands.

190. On August 16th, 1807, **a British fleet demanded the surrender of the Danish fleet.**

191. **When their demand was rejected, the British began to fire on the city,** killing two hundred or more civilians and over three thousand sailors and soldiers. The siege lasted until September 7th, 1807.

192. **Britain was heavily criticized for attacking a neutral country,** but the attack had its desired effect and kept Denmark from joining Napoleon in his war against England.

193. **At the Battle of Køge Bay in late August 1807, Danish forces managed to inflict greater casualties on British forces.** The Danish lost the battle, though, which helped remove Denmark from Napoleon's influence until **the Napoleonic Wars ended in 1815.**

194. By 1814, **Napoleon had been defeated and exiled from France.** He returned briefly in 1815 until his final defeat at Waterloo on June 19th, 1815.

195. **The Napoleonic Wars had a devastating effect on Denmark.** It lost around half its territory and suffered severe economic damage and hardship during these years, though it recovered surprisingly quickly.

196. **There were two kings of Denmark during the Napoleonic Wars: Christian VII,** who ruled an amazing forty-two years (r. 1766–1808), and **Frederick VI** (r. 1808–1839).

197. **The Danish defeats during the Napoleonic Wars made most Danes realize that their small size would mean they would no longer be a great power in Europe.**

198. In the modern day, **there are many artifacts from the period on display at some museums across Europe that document the Napoleonic Wars,** including weapons, uniforms, and documents at Denmark's National Museum.

199. Today, **England and Denmark are close political, economic, and military allies,** but it took almost a century for the Danes to fully trust the British again.

200. **The French Revolution and the Napoleonic Wars gave birth to modern nationalism throughout Europe,** which would later be a major contributing factor to World War One.

The Loss of Norway to Sweden
(1814–1815)

This chapter will explore the dramatic events of how and when Denmark lost Norway to Sweden. Let's take a look at several engaging facts about this period.

201. In 1814, **Denmark and Norway were both part of the same kingdom ruled by King Frederick VI.**

202. **After the Napoleonic Wars, Sweden saw a chance to finally claim Norway,** which had been historically tied to Denmark.

203. **King Frederick signed the Treaty of Kiel with Sweden,** which officially led to the loss of Norway.

204. **This treaty officially ended the Napoleonic Wars in Denmark.**

205. While all of **Norway became part of Sweden, Denmark retained Greenland, the Faroe Islands, and Iceland.**

206. **The Norwegians fought for their independence** or at least greater autonomy.

207. **Norway was weaker militarily and faced a swift defeat by Sweden.**

208. **The war only lasted a few months,** ending in August 1814.

209. **Norway and Sweden eventually entered into a personal union,** resulting in a unique relationship. For instance, Norway had its own constitution.

210. Historians call this conflict various names, with the most accepted being **the Swedish-Norwegian War.**

211. **Norway remained part of Sweden until 1905.** It was dissolved peacefully and ended over arguments about foreign policy.

212. **The loss of Norway meant that Sweden gained access to Danish resources and strategic positions.** This impacted the Danish economy in a negative way.

213. **Despite all these setbacks, Denmark still managed to remain an important trading nation** thanks to the large merchant fleet it built up during this timeframe.

214. **The loss of Norway resulted in a new wave of nationalism among citizens from both Denmark and Sweden.** Many Norwegians felt that it was time for them to have their own country independent of either Sweden or Denmark.

215. **Denmark undertook military reforms after 1814 in response to losing Norway and the shifting political landscape in Europe.** The Danish military saw efforts to modernize both the army and navy, although these were limited by economic constraints.

216. **Denmark improved its fortifications, notably in Copenhagen,** which had played a role in the Napoleonic Wars and would play a role in later conflicts.

217. **Denmark's policy began to lean more toward neutrality** rather than forming new strategic military alliances. **Denmark focused on defending its remaining territories** rather than engaging in alliances that could draw it into further conflicts.

218. **Denmark's neutrality allowed it to concentrate on internal affairs and development,** avoiding the economic and social tolls of major wars.

219. **Denmark, Norway, and Sweden have grown closer since then,** with close economic and military cooperation between all three countries.

220. **Even today, many Danes feel connected to Norwegian culture and customs due to shared history and language.** These special ties bind them together despite being separate nations.

Industrial Revolution in Denmark
(1800–1900)

This chapter **will explore the remarkable period of industrialization in Denmark between 1800 and 1900.** We'll uncover twenty interesting facts about this era, such as how new technologies enabled a shift from an agricultural economy to one that was largely dependent on industry.

221. In the early 1800s, **Denmark was primarily an agricultural country** with limited industrialization.

222. **The first modern factories appeared in the 1830s and 1840s.** They mainly produced textiles like cotton cloth and woolen fabrics. This marked the early stages of industrialization in the country.

223. **Around the middle of the 19th century, new technologies allowed for more efficient production of goods,** such as paper, iron products, and ceramics.

224. **Steam engines were introduced in the late 1840s to help power industrial processes,** such as spinning yarn and sawing lumber.

225. **With increased capital funding from investors, businesses could expand their operations quickly**, which led to rapid industrialization throughout Denmark. Businesses could invest in new technologies, expand production capacities, and contribute to the country's overall industrial development.

226. By 1860, perhaps **a thousand or more companies were operating in Denmark in various industries,** including shipping and transportation.

227. **Railroads began connecting cities all across Denmark** by 1864, allowing them to transport manufactured goods more efficiently.

228. In the 1860s, **Denmark became one of the first countries to develop a comprehensive public education system and free healthcare for its citizens.**

229. **Women and children began working in factories during this time as well,** which helped fuel industrial production further but resulted in widespread abuse.

230. **Despite a short but disastrous military defeat at the hands of Prussia in 1864,** Denmark's economy grew throughout the 19th century. Per capita income grew about 400 percent from 1840 to 1890.

231. In the late 19th century, **the Danish government introduced labor laws** that regulated hours, wages, and workplace safety.

232. In 1902, **Denmark did not allow children under twelve to work in factories.**

233. By 1880, over **25 percent of Danes were employed by industries** rather than agriculture.

234. **Industrialization led to an increase in the urban population due to people moving from farming communities and looking for job opportunities elsewhere.** This led cities like Copenhagen to expand rapidly throughout the 19th century.

235. Throughout Europe, but especially in western Europe, **railroads allowed people to easily visit or move to other parts of their own countries,** something that might take days or even weeks by foot or carriage.

236. **Railroads allowed more people to easily travel to other countries**, increasing the flow of information and building a more cosmopolitan society.

237. **Increased foreign trade meant imported goods** (such as coal) became cheaper, while exports (like butter) saw increased demand abroad.

238. In the late 1800s, **new technologies such as electricity and gas lamps were developed** to further facilitate industrial production and produce a profound change in society, creating a "nightlife."

239. **Advances in communication and transportation technology, like the telegraph and railroad,** allowed for greater coordination between factories across Denmark, enabling them to produce goods more efficiently than ever before and to gain information about new technological advances in the newly industrialized countries of western Europe.

240. By 1900, **Denmark was no longer a predominantly agricultural country** relying on manufactured imports but a major exporter of manufactured items.

The Schleswig Wars with Prussia and Austria (1848–1864)

The First Schleswig War and the Second Schleswig War were pivotal conflicts in Denmark's history, centering on the contested territory of Schleswig-Holstein. Let's look at twenty-five intriguing facts about these wars.

241. **The First Schleswig War** (1848–1850) **began due to disputes over the status of Schleswig and Holstein,** which were part of the Danish monarchy but had a predominantly German-speaking population.

242. **Conflicting claims led to Danish attempts to fully integrate these regions,** sparking a rebellion and conflict with the German Confederation.

243. **At the time of the war, Prussia was one of the two dominant powers** (the other being Austria) in what is now Germany.

244. **Prussian and other German nobles had claims to lands near and over the Danish border** where Schleswig, Holstein, and Lauenberg were.

245. **Many German-speaking people felt that the Danish government treated them like second-class citizens and wanted to join the other German-speaking states,** which is one reason war broke out at this time.

246. In the first war, **the Danes fought the Prussians to a standstill, but their troops were exhausted.** The two sides finally negotiated a peace called the London Protocol.

247. **The agreement spelled out that Denmark was not the owner of these regions. The Danish king, Frederick VII, was the duke of these three territories.** For complicated diplomatic reasons, both sides agreed to this.

248. In 1864, **Prussian Chancellor Otto von Bismarck, as part of his plan to unite all Germans under the Prussian Crown, provoked a war with Denmark and its king, Christian IX,** over the three duchies.

249. Austria joined Prussia because it also had influence in the region.

250. Denmark had no chance of victory against these two larger powers, but the Danish army and navy fought hard for nearly nine months before they had to ask for peace terms.

251. In 1864, **the Treaty of Vienna, which followed the Danish military defeat,** caused Denmark to lose all three territories.

252. Schleswig, the more northern area, was given to Prussia, and Holstein was given to Austria. This worked in Bismarck's favor, as the Austrian-controlled land would be between Prussia and Schleswig.

253. Bismarck planned to engineer an excuse about Austrian interference in allowing Prussian supplies to go through its territory so Prussia could eliminate Austrian influence from the German-speaking states.

254. The Austro-Prussian War started in 1866, less than two years after the war with Denmark officially ended.

255. In 1866, **Schleswig and Holstein officially became part of Germany,** with Lauenberg given to **Bismark** as his own personal estate by **Kaiser Wilhelm I.**

256. In 1871, **Prussia won a war with France, the only other nation with great influence in the German states.** This allowed the Prussian royal family to become the rulers of a united Germany. This move would have profound consequences for Denmark, Scandinavia, and the rest of the world.

257. Though it's sometimes difficult for Norwegians and Swedes to understand Danes, the Scandinavian languages are mutually intelligible, meaning they can be understood by most people in those countries. However, German and Danish, while both being from the same language family, are not. This and other issues caused many Danes to move out of the lost territories into Denmark.

258. After WWI, **an international conference supervised a vote in Schleswig.** Virtually all of the Danes still in the northern part of Schleswig voted to reunify with Denmark.

259. **A part of northern Schleswig was returned to Denmark. It is now called South Jutland.**

260. In some parts of Southern Jutland (Sønderjylland) **that were historically part of the Danish Duchy of Schleswig and under German rule** for periods of time, there is a German-speaking minority.

261. **On the German side of the border, particularly in the region of North Schleswig (Nordschleswig), there is a Danish-speaking minority.** There are Danish language schools and cultural centers there.

262. **In border areas and cities like Flensburg, bilingualism is common,** with most residents being fluent in **both Danish and German. Both languages have had historical and cultural influence in the region.** Those who don't speak one another's language often communicate in English.

263. **Today, Denmark and Germany are close allies despite their turbulent past together.**

264. The 1864 **war with Germany caused Denmark to come to terms with its size and reduced influence.**

265. Until **1949, when it joined NATO,** Denmark attempted to remain neutral.

WWI and WWII: Neutrality and Invasion
(1914–1945)

Explore the significant role Denmark played during WWI and WWII. We'll take a look at several interesting facts about Denmark's declaration of neutrality, its involvement in **the Battle of Jutland,** and much more!

266. **Denmark declared neutrality in World War I** on August 1st, 1914.

267. At the start of the war, **Denmark had only ten thousand men in its army** and just fifteen naval combat ships.

268. **The British and German armies numbered in the millions.** Both the British Royal Navy and the German Kriegsmarine had dozens of large combat vessels at their disposal.

269. **German and British naval forces clashed off the coast of the Danish region of Jutland** in 1916 because Germany was trying to blockade Britain from its supplies.

270. **Jutland was the biggest naval battle of WWI,** but it ended in what most historians consider a stalemate.

271. **Despite being neutral, Denmark allowed German submarines** (U-boats) **passage through its waters.**

272. Even though allowing German U-boats in Danish waters seemed to break neutrality, **the Danish government argued that it was necessary to allow German U-boats to dock in order to avoid conflict with Germany.**

273. **The number of German U-boats that docked at Danish ports is unknown,** but it is estimated that over one hundred U-boats did so during the war.

274. **The U-boats typically stayed in Danish ports for a few days,** during which time they refueled and repaired.

275. **Denmark also mined the waters around much of its territory.** They did this with the encouragement of the British, who knew the minefields would prevent or slow the movement of German warships from the Baltic Sea.

276. **The geographic position of Denmark was very important to military strategy at the time.** It gave Denmark more power than its size shows.

277. **The Danes still play an important role in the area, especially within NATO.**

278. **Germany tried using diplomatic pressure on Denmark** in 1918, which failed due to strong public opposition against Denmark becoming involved in active warfare.

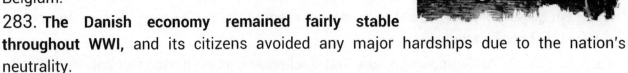

279. During WWI, **Denmark welcomed refugees from both Allied and Central Power nations like Germany and Russia.**

280. **The Danish government established a number of refugee camps to provide shelter and food for refugees.** The government also provided refugees with financial assistance and helped them to find work.

281. **The Danish people also helped refugees by opening their homes** to them and providing them with clothing and other necessities.

282. **The number of refugees who came to Denmark during World War I is unknown,** but it is estimated that over ten thousand refugees came to Denmark during the war. The refugees came from a variety of countries, including Germany, Russia, Austria-Hungary, and Belgium.

283. **The Danish economy remained fairly stable throughout WWI,** and its citizens avoided any major hardships due to the nation's neutrality.

284. When WWII began in 1939, **Denmark declared it would remain neutral again but was unable to maintain it due to the German invasion** on April 9th, 1940.

285. During WWII (1941–1945), **more than 4,500 Danes served voluntarily or with the Allied forces,** having fled during or after the German invasion.

The Interwar Years
(1918–1939)

Between 1918 and 1939, Denmark experienced a dynamic period marked by a series of significant events. In these two decades, **Denmark** navigated an evolving geopolitical landscape, **fostering social progress and adaptation to external political pressures.** Let's take a look at twenty facts about this period.

286. **Before the interwar years, in 1915, Danish women gained the right to vote,** marking a milestone in gender equality and democratic participation.

287. Denmark's neutral stance during World War I ended with the war's conclusion in 1918.

288. In 1920, **Denmark became a member of the League of Nations, actively participating in international diplomacy and peacekeeping efforts.** This membership underscored Denmark's commitment to maintaining global peace and cooperation following the tumultuous years of World War I.

289. **The 1920s witnessed the emergence of nationalist movements** in response to political and economic challenges, shaping Denmark's domestic landscape.

290. **Denmark, like the rest of the world, grappled with economic difficulties brought on by the Great Depression.**

291. In the 1920s, **Denmark introduced various social reforms,** including labor laws, to enhance the well-being of its citizens.

292. Frequent changes in government during **the 1920s reflected Denmark's political instability caused by economic challenges.**

293. **Responding to political and economic issues,** nationalist groups gained prominence, influencing **Danish society.**

294. **Denmark actively worked to expand international trade relationships,** recognizing the importance of global commerce.

295. **Constitutional adjustments were made during the 1930s,** affecting Denmark's political landscape.

Nazi Occupation of Denmark
(1940–1945)

Explore the tragic but remarkable story of the Nazi occupation in Denmark. Discover twenty-five intriguing facts about how ordinary Danish citizens lived under Nazi rule.

296. On April 9th, 1940, **Nazi Germany invaded Denmark and occupied the country for the next five years.** Denmark was occupied until the very last days of the war.

297. **Danish King Christian X refused to cooperate with Germany's demands but decided not to fight against them.** He wanted to spare his people from violence and destruction.

298. **Though the Danish people suffered under Nazi rule,** Hitler's ideas of race gave Denmark more leeway to deal with its own affairs during the war.

299. **Hitler believed that, along with the Germans, Danes and other Scandinavians were the embodiment of the so-called "Aryan master race."**

300. **Laws were enacted in Denmark that saw the Jewish population essentially removed from public life.** They could not hold most jobs or positions within the government.

301. **The harsh laws pushed many Danes to resist Nazi rule either on their own in small ways or with the many resistance groups** that sprung up throughout Denmark.

302. In August 1943, **Denmark was declared an official protectorate by Nazi Germany.**

303. **The Danish resistance movement started almost immediately after the occupation began.** It promoted nonviolence at first and later **engaged in sabotage activities,** such as strikes, boycotts, and distributing underground newspapers.

304. **Resistance activities also included violence against Danish collaborators** and, on occasion, Nazi forces.

305. **Denmark, Great Britain, and, to a lesser degree, the US used neutral Sweden as a place to meet, coordinate, and secretly supply the Danish resistance.**

306. In October 1943, a daring **rescue mission was undertaken, during which over 7,200 Jewish refugees,** along with nearly 700 non-Jewish spouses, were smuggled out of Denmark aboard fishing boats across the Baltic Sea to neutral Sweden.

307. **The Danish government managed to negotiate with the Germans for food and supplies during the occupation,** which allowed most Danes to avoid starvation and malnutrition, unlike other occupied countries in Europe.

308. In October 1944, **a general strike was organized by the resistance movement that lasted two days, shutting down all transportation networks and forcing Nazi Germany to declare martial law in Denmark as punishment.**

309. **A curfew was imposed on citizens throughout much of 1944,** restricting their movements between certain hours each day or night, depending on what region they lived in.

310. **The Nazis enforced censorship of newspapers, books, and other media during their occupation of Denmark,** controlling what information could be released to the public.

311. **Some ships of the Royal Danish Navy managed to escape to Great Britain,** lending their strength to the Allied war effort. However, most of the Danish fleet could not escape and was scuttled before they could fall into Nazi hands.

312. **Members of extremist right-wing Danish groups, including the Danish Nazi Party, formed the Schalburg Corps,** which was used by the Germans to hunt down rebels and work as police enforcers.

313. **Another six thousand or so Danes volunteered for the Waffen-SS,** the armed branch of **Heinrich Himmler's** dreaded SS.

314. In May 1945, **after five years of Nazi rule in Denmark, Allied forces liberated Copenhagen,** which brought an end to German control over the country.

315. **The liberation did not include any significant fighting,** as most Germans were either retreating back to Germany while they could or simply gave up, knowing the war was lost.

316. **The liberation was celebrated by many Danes across the nation,** with citizens parading down streets rejoicing at their regained freedom.

317. **When Germany surrendered, there were about 250,000 German refugees in Denmark** who had fled from the Eastern Front. Many were given homes or Danish schools to stay in, causing great resentment in Denmark.

318. **At the end of the war, complicated negotiations took place between the Danes and the Allied governments,** allowing most of the German refugees to return to Germany.

319. **During these five years under occupation, around 6,500 Danes died,** either through executions, because they lost their lives fighting against Nazis, or from simply trying to survive the harsh conditions imposed upon the country.

320. In 1950, **Ryvangen Memorial Park was established not far outside Copenhagen.** It is dedicated to the men and women who fought and died in the resistance during WWII.

The Postwar Period
(1945–the 1960s)

Discover **the remarkable changes that took place in Denmark after World War II** with this chapter's exploration of twenty interesting facts about the postwar period.

321. In 1945, **Denmark was liberated from Nazi occupation.** It became a democratic constitutional monarchy, with a new constitution reinforcing democratic institutions and laws.

322. **The first postwar elections to the Danish Parliament were held in 1947.** The Social Democrats won the majority of votes.

323. **The Danish Social Democratic Party was a prominent political force** known for its progressive policies and contributions to the country's postwar rebuilding efforts.

324. **The Social Democrats won due to their popular policies,** postwar reconstruction agenda, leadership under **Hans Hedtoft,** and ability to provide political stability and economic recovery after World War II.

325. **Though Denmark suffered during WWII, it avoided the large-scale destruction other nations faced,** which helped Denmark's postwar economy.

326. **By 1951, almost all Danish households had access to electricity,** thanks to an ambitious electric grid project funded by taxes as part of economic recovery efforts after WWII ended.

327. Between 1953 and 1960, **there was a housing boom across Denmark, which saw more than 800,000 dwellings built**.

328. In 1960, **Denmark joined the European Free Trade Association (EFTA),** making it easier to trade with other countries in western Europe and creating more jobs in Danish industries.

329. **The first Danish television station was launched by Danmarks Radio or "DR"** (known as Danish Broadcasting Corporation in English) in 1951, bringing entertainment into homes across Denmark.

330. **During this period, a lot of investments were made in better education,** leading to an increase in literacy rates among young people and adults.

331. **University enrollment also increased significantly,** which led to improvements in research and development in many different fields, including medicine, technology, agriculture, etc.

332. After the war, many nations in western Europe, including **Denmark, began to build a more comprehensive system of social security** that provided financial support for people who were unable to work due to illness or disability.

333. **Denmark experienced significant advancements in public transportation infrastructure.** The government invested in modernizing and expanding the rail and road networks, making travel more efficient and accessible to the public.

334. **Urban areas saw the growth of tram and bus services, improving local transportation** options and contributing to Denmark's economic and social development during this era.

335. **In 1967, all Danes had access to healthcare** through government-funded hospitals and doctors' offices. It is one of the best public healthcare systems in the world today. These programs are largely paid for by Denmark's higher than average tax rates.

336. **During these years, there was an influx of immigrants from countries like Turkey, Pakistan, and Morocco.**

337. **The postwar period saw a transition from subsistence farming to industrial agriculture,** as well as an improvement in food production technology with the introduction of new technologies and methods.

338. **In 1954, Denmark, Sweden, Norway, and Iceland formed a Scandinavian trade bloc known as the Nordic Passport Union.** It allows the citizens of these countries to travel freely without a passport or a visa.

339. **The 1960s saw Denmark become a more open-minded society,** with increasing social acceptance of divorce, homosexuality, and women's rights.

340. **During these years, there was an increase in environmental awareness and efforts to protect nature,** with new regulations introduced to reduce pollution from factories or other activities.

The Cold War and NATO Membership
(1949–Present)

This chapter will explore **the fascinating history of Denmark's participation in the Cold War and its membership in NATO.** Let's take a look at twenty interesting facts about this period.

341. In 1949, **Denmark became one of the first countries in the world to join NATO** (the North Atlantic Treaty Organization). It has remained a member ever since.

342. **NATO was created to counter the threat of invasion into Western Europe by the Soviet Union** and its Eastern European allies.

343. **After joining NATO in 1949, Denmark became increasingly involved with international security efforts within Europe as well as abroad.**

344. From 1963 to 1965, **Danish forces took part in United Nations peacekeeping operations** during conflicts in Cyprus and the Congo's civil war.

345. **The Danish Navy and a large number of land-based missile batteries,** sea mines, and anti-submarine devices are in place in the straits that lead from the Baltic Sea to the North Sea and the Atlantic.

346. **Denmark continues to play an important role in observing and following the movement of Russian ships moving from one place to another in the Baltic area.**

347. Throughout much of the 1990s, **Denmark and the other NATO member states experienced a pause in military tensions with the Soviet Union.**

348. **The easing of tensions between Western and Eastern Europe after the Cold War meant that Denmark began to spend less of its national budget on its military.**

349. By 1992, **all Danish forces had been withdrawn from West Germany,** which marked an official end to its participation in Cold War operations there.

350. **Denmark also participated in missions such as the United Nations Interim Force during Lebanon's civil war** from 1982 to 1985, **the Stabilization Force for Bosnia and Herzegovina** from 1996 to 2004, and **the Kosovo Force** in 1999.

351. **From 2001 to 2003, Danish troops participated in Operation Enduring Freedom,** which involved actions against terrorism in Afghanistan.

352. In 2001, **Denmark took part in NATO's mission in Afghanistan** when it joined **the International Security Assistance Force** (ISAF) to help keep peace and stability after the fall of the Taliban regime.

353. From 2012 to 2014, **Danish forces were deployed to Mali as part of a UN peacekeeping mission** aimed at restoring order and providing humanitarian aid following a coup d'état there.

354. Since 2014, **the Royal Danish Air Force has supported anti-ISIS operations** by launching airstrikes from bases located throughout the Middle East.

355. Amid growing tensions with Russia, in 2018, **Danish soldiers participated in Exercise Trident Juncture,** the largest military exercise in Norway since the end of the Cold War. This exercise included nearly fifty thousand NATO soldiers, sailors, and airmen, including one thousand Danes.

356. **The militaries of Denmark, Norway, and Sweden, especially their navies and air forces, work closely together,** given their proximity and close ties.

357. As of 2021, **over fifty Danish soldiers have been killed in action during peacekeeping missions.** Though that's a relatively small number, it should be remembered that Denmark is a very small country with a relatively small population.

358. **Danish ships and military personnel have routinely been sent to the Mediterranean to help with the refugee crisis** that has been going on since 2015.

359. In 2018, **Danish forces were deployed as part of a European Union mission known as Operation Sophia,** which aims at combating piracy off **the coast of Somalia** and protecting maritime trade routes.

360. Today, **Denmark continues its involvement with NATO operations** through both onshore presence (such as training exercises) and offshore combat missions (like air strikes against ISIS).

Immigration to Denmark
(the 1960s–Present)

This chapter will explore the history of immigration in Denmark from the 1960s to the present day. We'll delve into twenty interesting facts about how laws and regulations have changed over time, as well as what impact these changes have had on Danish society.

361. Since the 1960s, **Denmark has had some of the most liberal immigration laws in Europe.**

362. **Denmark**, like many of the northern European countries, **has been a major destination for people trying to escape** persecution, repression, or war in their homelands.

363. **Migrants from Turkey, Yugoslavia, and Pakistan increasingly began to arrive in Denmark** for work opportunities in the 1960s.

364. **The Danish Aliens Act of 1972 granted residence permits to those considered likely to contribute positively to Danish society or the economy,** such as family reunification cases or skilled workers in professions like engineering and healthcare.

365. In 1978, **temporary guest worker programs were introduced, allowing individuals outside the EU areas access to short-term employment contracts in industrial sectors,** such as construction and food production.

366. During the 1980s, **large numbers of refugees sought asylum,** often due to civil war conflicts occurring in the Middle East.

367. The year 1991 **saw extended rights given to foreign nationals living permanently within state borders,** allowing them access to public services and to gain some of same rights and protections as Danish citizens.

368. **The Immigration Act of 1998 saw changes made that allowed for more flexible family reunification laws,** with the removal of most language and educational requirements for spouses joining their families in Denmark.

369. In 2002, **the Integration Law was passed, aiming to help immigrants better assimilate into society** by providing language classes and job training initiatives.

370. In 2003, **asylum seekers were granted work permits after six months of residence in the country,** which meant they could begin contributing positively to the economy while waiting for their permanent resident applications to be processed.

371. In the late 2000s and 2010s, **there was a considerable backlash in Denmark against the**

Muslim practice of women face coverings. Some believed masking the face was a security threat, while others believed the practice had no place in Denmark.

372. Since 2018, **there has been a ban in place against women's face coverings in public spaces, but it is seldom enforced.**

373. On December 12th, 2008, **new rules were introduced, making it easier for individuals outside the EU to obtain a residence permit** if they had worked in Denmark two years before the application date.

374. In 2010, **several points systems regarding immigration from third-party nations were introduced.** Applicants were awarded higher points based on desired skills and language capabilities. **The points system was introduced** in response to concerns about Denmark's aging population and declining workforce.

375. In 2011, **a new program was created to let people from outside the EU come and work in Denmark** if they had certain qualifications, like having a job offer and making 375,000 Danish kroner or more. This was largely aimed at gaining skilled workers in tech and workers from more technologically advanced nations.

376. From 2014 to 2015, **the number of asylum seekers entering Denmark rose significantly** due to the political turmoil occurring in the Middle East.

377. In 2016, **a new immigration law was introduced aiming to reduce rights in family reunification cases,** with stricter educational and language provisions placed on spouses wanting to join their families in the country. **This law made it more challenging for some individuals to join their families in Denmark,** and it generated considerable debate.

378. In 2017, **right-wing nationalist groups rose throughout Europe,** resulting in greater amounts of anti-immigration rhetoric being spread among the population. **However, the majority still support allowing immigration,** albeit with more restrictions than before 2015.

379. In August 2018, **reforms to the Immigration Act of 1998 were made, which allowed foreign nationals more options for finding jobs in Denmark.**

380. **Comparatively speaking, Denmark has seen fewer issues arising from the massive wave of immigration than other western European countries,** but it forced the country to question its previously welcoming immigration policies.

EU Accession
(1973–1993)

This chapter **will explore the history of Denmark's accession to the European Union,** from its signing of the Maastricht Treaty to its referendum on EU membership in 2015.

381. Denmark joined the EEC, **the European Economic Community,** the precursor to today's EU, in 1973.

382. **The process of forming the modern-day EU** (European Union) began in earnest in 1992 when the Treaty of Maastricht was signed in the Netherlands.

383. **For Denmark to become part of the "new" EU under the Treaty of Maastricht,** which set up the European Union as an official governing and diplomatic body, not simply an economic union, a referendum had to be held where Danish citizens would decide if they wanted their country to join or not.

384. On June 2nd, 1992, **Danish citizens rejected the Maastricht Treaty** by a narrow majority (50 percent).

385. **Denmark's second referendum, held on May 18th, 1993, saw Danish citizens approve of the terms of the Maastricht Treaty** with certain opt-outs.

386. **Candidate countries must agree to abide by certain laws and regulations,** or acquis communautaire, before they can be admitted to the EU.

387. **The most moden version of the Schengen Agreement allows for free movement of people between all signatories,** meaning it is very easy for the citizens of EU countries to move, work, and live in other countries besides their own.

388. **Denmark is part of four main institutions within the European Union: the European Council,** the European Parliament, the Court of Justice of the European Union, and the Council of the European Union.

389. **Denmark is not a member of the European Central Bank** (ECB), having opted out of **the Economic and Monetary Union** (EMU).

390. **A key aspect of the Maastricht Treaty was based on creating economic stability across all member states,** which led to the introduction of a single currency (the euro) in 1999.

391. **Denmark was one of the first countries to sign up for opt-outs,** which means it does not have to **abide by some rules that are part of being an EU member state, such as using the euro.** Denmark uses the Danish krone.

392. **Since Denmark joined the EEC in 1973, its trade with other EU countries has increased significantly.** At the moment, EU nations are Denmark's largest group of trade partners.

393. **EU membership has also given Denmark access to larger and more plentiful money and resources,** which has allowed it to make important improvements to farming, transportation, and much else.

394. In 2021, **there were fourteen Danish representatives to the European Parliament from the following Danish political parties: four Social Democrats,** four from Venstre, four **from the Danish People's Party,** and one each **from the Conservative People's Party** and **the Socialist People's Party.** These represent moderate, left-wing, and right-wing parties in Denmark.

395. **Denmark's membership in the EU has resulted in economic benefits** hovering around ten billion euros a year (approximately 10.5 billion US dollars in 2023).

396. **Though Denmark exports many types of products, especially delicious food, to other EU members and the world, machinery is the number one Danish export to other EU nations.** That sector is worth over twenty billion euros and accounts for nearly 30 percent of Denmark's exports.

397. **Denmark is an active member of the European Union and participates in many important decisions,** such as trade agreements, foreign policy initiatives, and climate change programs.

398. **The Maastricht Treaty also established the "Three Pillars" of the EU,** which are economic and social cooperation, common foreign and security policy, and cooperation in justice and home affairs.

399. **Being in NATO and the EU has allowed Denmark to magnify its small territory and population and increase its power and influence,** especially in regard to non-EU countries.

400. **Since joining the EU, Denmark has become one of the most prosperous (and happiest) countries in Europe,** with high levels of employment and a strong economy.

Growth in Tourism
(1980–Present)

This chapter will explore the remarkable growth in tourism that Denmark experienced between 1980 and the 2020s.

401. **In 1980, eight million tourists visited Denmark. By 2010, that number had increased to ten million,** according to UNWTO, the UN World Tourism Organization.

402. **In the 1980s, the country was known mostly for its picturesque landscapes and charming towns,** which helped attract visitors from many countries around the world.

403. **Copenhagen became one of Europe's most popular cities due to its historic sites and nightlife attractions like Tivoli Gardens,** the world's second-oldest amusement park.

404. **The Ny Carlsberg Glyptotek is a renowned museum in Copenhagen, Denmark,** featuring an extensive **collection of ancient and modern art, including Egyptian, Greek, Roman, and Etruscan artifacts,** as well as Danish and French sculptures and paintings, with works by artists like Rodin and Gauguin.

405. **Viking culture saw a resurgence in popularity in the 2000s and the 2010s, with reenactments throughout Denmark** drawing large crowds who wanted to learn more about their heritage or simply have fun participating in the festivities.

406. **Statens Museum for Kunst,** located in Copenhagen, Denmark, is the national gallery, housing a vast collection of Danish and international art from the past seven centuries. One can find masterpieces by **Mantegna, Rembrandt, and Picasso,** as well as a notable collection of works from **the Danish Golden Age** (the first half of the 19th century).

407. **The Little Mermaid statue located in Copenhagen became famous worldwide after Disney's movie was released.** Now, many people visit just to take pictures or admire its beauty. Many tourists are likely shocked at how small the statue is.

408. In the mid-2000s, **Danish cuisine, restaurants, and chefs began to be recognized** as some of the best and most innovative in the world on shows like **Anthony Bourdain's No Reservations,** Parts Unknown, and others.

409. **Today, tourism accounts for about 2.5 percent of Danish GDP and 4.1 percent of its employment.** This is expected to increase as the economy recovers from the 2020 pandemic.

410. **For many years, Denmark has been voted one of the most livable countries in Europe** (and the world) due to its high-quality infrastructure and well-developed public services, making it even more attractive for travelers looking for a getaway.

411. **One of the many attractions for English speakers is that Denmark has a very high number of English speakers.** Since the Danish language is only spoken by Danes, who number less than the city of New York, most Danes learn English, German, or both as a second language.

412. **To accommodate the increase in visitors, many hotels were built throughout the country,** offering guests luxurious amenities, such as beachfront views or spas.

413. In 2016, **Denmark was ranked the second happiest country in the world according to the World Happiness Report,** which further helped increase its popularity with tourists.

414. **With the rise of vacation homestays and the ability to stay and participate on a working Danish farm,** more and more tourists are branching out and not just visiting Copenhagen.

415. **Some of the most visited sites in Denmark were built nearly 1,500 years ago.** The Viking ring fortresses, sometimes called **trelleborgs** for a town where one lies, are increasingly popular tourists sites. **There are five trelleborgs in Denmark, two in Sweden,** and two more likely fortresses being examined in Sweden and Norway.

Renewable Energy Initiatives
(1990s–Present)

Since the 1990s, **Denmark has been at the forefront of renewable energy initiatives,** and their commitment to sustainability is inspiring. This chapter will explore twenty fascinating facts about **Denmark's renewable energy efforts** from 1996 to 2021.

416. In 1996, **the Parliament of Denmark passed the world's first law to promote renewable energy sources.**

417. **Denmark is now a world leader in renewable energy.** In 2020, renewable energy accounted for 60 percent of Denmark's total energy consumption.

418. In 1997, **14 percent of the electricity produced in Denmark came from wind power,** one of the highest levels in Europe at that time.

419. **According to the Danish Energy Agency, by 2004, almost 20 percent of all electricity used in Denmark was generated by wind turbines** and other forms of renewable energy, such as solar and biomass resources.

420. In 2006, **Copenhagen opened a waste-to-energy plant that used household trash to create heat and hot water.**

421. **Pipes filled with hot water generated from waste-to-energy plants were placed under some of Copenhagen's busiest streets,** causing snow to melt in the winter, reducing the need for polluting snowplows.

422. As of 2016, **Denmark had three experimental wave power stations working on harnessing the power of the ocean for energy.**

423. **The year 2008 saw more than 25 percent of the total production of electricity from renewable energy sources;** this was the highest in Europe at the time.

424. In 2010, **Denmark set a world record for wind power, generating more than 30 percent of its electricity from that form of renewable energy.**

425. **Most of Denmark is coastline,** and it benefits from almost constant wind coming from the sea.

426. In 2011, **Copenhagen's city council passed legislation to become carbon neutral by 2025,** using only renewable energy resources, such as solar and wind power, to meet its targets.

427. **Copenhagen wants to become the world's most livable city and is investing heavily in green infrastructure projects** like bike lanes, electric buses, and district heating systems powered entirely by renewable energy sources.

428. In 2015, **Apple opened a data center near Viborg, which uses 100 percent renewable energy supplied from nearby wind farms and biomass facilities,** providing clean electricity back to local communities.

429. **While often cited as a model for clean energy and climate sense, it should be remembered that while Denmark is technologically innovative,** it is a small country with fewer competing interests, like the oil industry in the United States.

430. In 2020, **Denmark committed to reducing its greenhouse gas emissions 70 percent below 1990 levels by 2030,** setting itself up to be a global leader in sustainability.

431. **In 2021, the government announced its plan to produce enough clean energy from offshore wind farms by 2025** to power over six million homes.

432. **Denmark plans to build the world's biggest artificial island in the North Sea** powered entirely by renewable energy sources like wind and solar.

433. **The island will be located about eighty kilometers off the coast of Denmark** and will be connected to the mainland by electricity cables.

434. **The island will be built using sand and gravel dredged from the seabed and will be protected from the sea by a surrounding dike.**

435. In 2023, **Copenhagen's harbor began construction of its new green ports, aiming for zero emissions from all vessels** entering or leaving its docks using only 100 percent clean energy.

Digitization and Technology in the 21st Century
(the 1990s–Present)

This chapter will explore the remarkable development of digitalization and technology in Denmark from the 1990s until the present day. Let's take a look at twenty-five important facts about how this small country was able to adopt advanced technologies.

436. In 2006, **Denmark experimented with a trial period of digital streaming.** In 2009, digital TV began nationwide.

437. **The Danish government invested heavily in broadband networks** in the 1990s, which made it possible for more households to access broadband internet.

438. **In 2000, Denmark launched its domain name system (.dk),** which allowed businesses and individuals in the country to have their website addresses on an international scale.

439. **The Danish government began using electronic public service systems (EPSS) in 2001,** allowing citizens easy access to essential information about healthcare, education, and more.

440. **The Danish government has been a leader in the development and implementation of EPSS,** and its success has served as a model for other countries around the world.

441. Since 2002, **mobile phones have been widely used by Danes, making it easier for them to stay connected with family and friends** abroad and in the country through calls, texts, and emails.

442. In 2002, **Denmark had over 3.5 million mobile phone subscriptions, which was equivalent to over 60 percent of the population.**

443. **By 2023, the number of mobile phone subscriptions in Denmark had increased to over 8.9 million, which is equivalent to over 150 percent of the population.** This means that most Danes have more than one mobile phone subscription.

444. In 2003, **Copenhagen became one of the first cities in northern Europe to have free public Wi-Fi,** which allowed people to access the internet without any charges or subscriptions.

445. **Denmark is a leader in sustainable food production and consumption.** Many Danish restaurants and food stores buy only from sustainable sources.

446. According to a 2022 survey by **the Danish Agriculture and Food Council,** 92 percent of Danes are concerned about the sustainability of the food they eat.

447. By 2005, **all schools and libraries across Denmark were equipped with computers,** allowing students and teachers to use technology for educational purposes.

448. In 2006, **the Danish government created an e-ID system,** which allows Danish citizens and residents of Denmark to prove their **identity online** when making payments or using services safely over the internet.

449. In 2009, **Copenhagen Airport became one of the first airports around the globe to offer its passengers real-time flight information through wireless networks** so they could easily navigate their way within the airport while waiting for flights.

450. **By 2011, more than 80 percent of Danes were using smartphones regularly** due to the gradual decline in prices and increased availability of different mobile applications and platforms.

451. **The Digital Post system was launched in 2012, allowing citizens to receive official mail online** instead of sending it through the mail.

452. In 2013, **Copenhagen City Center was designated a "smart city"** for its use of advanced technologies like sensors and Wi-Fi networks to monitor traffic flow and pollution levels, making urban management more efficient.

453. In 2014, **Denmark became one of the first countries in Europe to have a nationwide network for digital radio** (DAB+), ensuring easy access and high-quality sound quality throughout the country.

454. By 2015, **Danes had started using mobile payment systems like Apple Pay and Google Wallet**, making it easier for them to purchase goods from stores without any physical cash transactions.

455. In 2018, **Denmark launched its first satellite into space. It was called Ørsted** (after renowned Danish scientist **Hans Christian Ørsted**).

456. **Ørsted is a micro-satellite that is used to conduct research and gather data about the environment in real time**, providing new insights into climate change.

457. **The national healthcare system adopted e-health initiatives in 2019,** which allowed patients to get their medical records and reports over the internet securely rather than having to physically visit hospitals again and again.

458. In 2020, **Danes started using robots and AI technologies like chatbots or virtual assistants** more often as part of their daily lives, helping them automate mundane tasks such as ordering food online and paying bills.

459. In 2010, **Denmark introduced NemID, a common secure login for both public and private services.** It has become a cornerstone of the country's digital infrastructure, **enabling secure access to online banking, government services,** and various other digital platforms.

460. **Andreas Mogensen was the first Dane in space in 2015,** flying with an European Space Agency mission to the International Space Station.

National Heroes and Danish Celebrities

Explore a captivating journey through the realms of Danish culture, entertainment, and sports with this list of iconic figures.

461. **Gorm the Old** (c. 936–958) was **the Danish king** who established the first unified Kingdom of Denmark.

462. **Cnut the Great** (c. 995–1035) was a **medieval king** who ruled over a North Sea empire that included England and Norway.

463. **Margrethe I** (1353–1412) was **the Danish queen** who played a key role in the unification of Denmark, Sweden, and Norway.

464. **Tycho Brahe** (1546–1601) was a prominent **astronomer and alchemist** known for meticulous night sky observations.

465. **Ole Rømer** (1644–1710) was a **Danish astronomer** known for his contributions to understanding the speed of light.

466. **Hans Christian Andersen** (1805–1875) was the renowned **author of fairy tales** and children's literature.

467. **Søren Kierkegaard** (1813–1855) was **a philosopher,** theologian, and poet known for existentialist philosophy.

468. **Georg Brandes** (1842–1927) was **a Danish literary critic and scholar.** Born in Copenhagen, Denmark, he is best known for his work promoting realism and naturalism in literature, influencing many prominent Scandinavian authors.

469. **Niels Finsen** (1860–1904) was **a physician** and scientist who won the Nobel Prize for pioneering phototherapy.

470. **Ejnar Hertzsprung** (1873–1967) was **an astronomer known for the Hertzsprung-Russell diagram** used to classify stars.

471. **Niels Bohr** (1885–1962) was **a Danish physicist** known for his foundational contributions to quantum theory and the model of the atom.

472. **Karen Blixen** (1885–1962) was a renowned **Danish author** famous for works like Out of Africa and Babette's Feast. She wrote under the pen name Isak Dinesen.

473. **Inge Lehmann** (1888–1993) was a **seismologist** who discovered Earth's inner core.

474. **Carl Theodor Dreyer** (1889–1968) was an **influential Danish film director** known for classics like The Passion of Joan of Arc and Ordet.

475. **Ole Kirk Christiansen** (1891–1958) was the founder of **the Lego Group,** the company that produces the world-famous LEGO toys. Born in Filskov, Denmark, he started the company in 1932, which originally manufactured wooden toys before introducing the iconic plastic interlocking bricks in 1949.

476. **Marie Hammer** (1907-2002) **meticulously researched tiny insects.** Her studies played a crucial role in supporting the theory of continental drift.

477. **Niels Kaj Jerne** (1911–1994) was **a Danish immunologist** who received the Nobel Prize in physiology or medicine.

478. **Mærsk Mc-Kinney Møller** (1913–2012) was a Danish shipping magnate and **owner of A.P. Moller-Maersk Group.**

479. **Erik Christian Haugaard** (1927–2009) was **a Danish author** known for children's and young adult books.

480. **Anders Fogh Rasmussen** (b. 1953) was the former **prime minister of Denmark and secretary-general of NATO.**

481. **Erik Balling** (1924–2005) was **a Danish filmmaker and director** known for Olsen-Banden (the Olsen Gang), a comedy film series.

482. **Morten Grunwald** (1934–2021) was **a Danish actor famous** for his role as Benny in Olsen-Banden.

483. **Dirch Passer** (1926–1980) was an **iconic Danish comedian** and actor who was celebrated for his contributions to Danish comedy.

484. **Mads Mikkelsen** (b. 1965) is **a renowned Danish actor** known for his roles in films like Casino Royale and the TV series Hannibal.

485. **Nikolaj Coster-Waldau** (b.1970) is **a Danish actor** famous for his role as Jaime Lannister in the TV series Game of Thrones.

486. **Lars Ulrich** (b. 1963) is **a drummer** and the co-founder of the legendary heavy metal band Metallica.

487. **Anders Trentemøller** (b. 1972) is **a Danish electronic music producer** and DJ recognized for his innovative music.

488. **Victor Borge** (1909–2000) is **a Danish comedian and musician.** He escaped from Denmark during World War II. When he became a major star, he brought international attention to Denmark.

489. **Nina Agdal** (b. 1992) is **a Danish model** known for her appearances in the Sports Illustrated Swimsuit Issue and other high-profile campaigns.

490. **Mikkel Kessler** (b. 1979) is **a Danish former professional boxer** known for his successful boxing career.

491. **Michael Laudrup** (b. 1964) is **a legendary Danish football** (soccer) player and manager known for his exceptional skills on the field.

492. **Nicklas Bendtner** (b. 1988) is **a Danish football striker** known for his international career and club football in Europe.

493. **Josephine Skriver** (b. 1993) is **a Danish-born supermodel.** She has been an advocate for LGBTQ rights and was born via IVF.

494. **Birgitte Hjort Sørensen** (b. 1982) is **a Danish actress** known for her roles in TV series like Borgen and Game of Thrones.

495. **Queen Margarethe II abdicated the Danish throne in 2024 after fifty-two years on the throne.** She was succeeded by her son **Frederik X.** Her abdication had to do with her being a senior citizen. She was the first Danish monarch to voluntarily abdicate the throne since 1146.

Danish Habits and Customs

If you travel to Denmark or any other country, it's good to familiarize yourself with the customs and habits of the people there. While Danes are among some of the most accepting people on Earth, it's still good to understand the country and people where you are going. **Here are five common customs in Denmark.**

496. **Fastelavn is a Danish carnival that is celebrated on the last Sunday before Ash Wednesday.** On Fastelavn, children dress up in costumes and go door to door singing songs.

497. **Cycling is a very popular mode of transportation in Denmark.** Many Danes cycle to work, school, and for leisure.

498. **Smørrebrød is a traditional Danish open-faced sandwich that is typically made with rye bread.** Toppings include meat, fish, cheese, and vegetables.

499. **Janteloven (the Law of Jante) is a Danish social code that emphasizes modesty and conformity.** It is based on the idea that everyone is equal and that no one should think they are better than anyone else.

500. **If you are in Denmark around Christmas, you should check out the Tivoli Christmas market**. The market features festive decorations, light displays, and various stalls selling holiday treats and crafts.

Conclusion

Throughout this book, we have explored the richness of Denmark's history. From its prehistory years to the present day, it has played a major role in many European conflicts and changes. **Colonialism, industrialization, and modern technological developments have proven that Denmark is an important nation,** not only in Europe but also globally.

We observed how Christianity altered life for Danish people, and we learned about their contributions during WWI and WWII, regardless of whether they were neutral or involved with the Allied forces.

Each chapter showed us how unique yet adaptable the Danes are by looking into topics such as Viking Age customs and beliefs. We took a look at their **culture and society,** including **the environmental efforts** undertaken by governmental agencies that drive society toward embracing **renewable energy incentives.**
It is safe to say that Denmark's history is one worth exploring. We hope you continue your quest for knowledge and **learn more about Denmark** in the future!

If you enjoyed this book, a review on Amazon would be greatly appreciated because it would mean a lot to hear from you.

To leave a review:

1. Open your camera app.
2. Point your mobile device at the QR code.
3. The review page will appear in your web browser.

Thanks for your support!

Welcome Aboard, Check Out This Limited-Time Free Bonus!

Ahoy, reader! Welcome to the Ahoy Publications family, and thanks for snagging a copy of this book! Since you've chosen to join us on this journey, we'd like to offer you something special.

Check out the link below for a FREE e-book filled with delightful facts about American History.

But that's not all - you'll also have access to our exclusive email list with even more free e-books and insider knowledge. Well, what are ye waiting for? Click the link below to join and set sail toward exciting adventures in American History.

Access your bonus here: https://ahoypublications.com/

Or, Scan the QR code!

Check out another book in the series

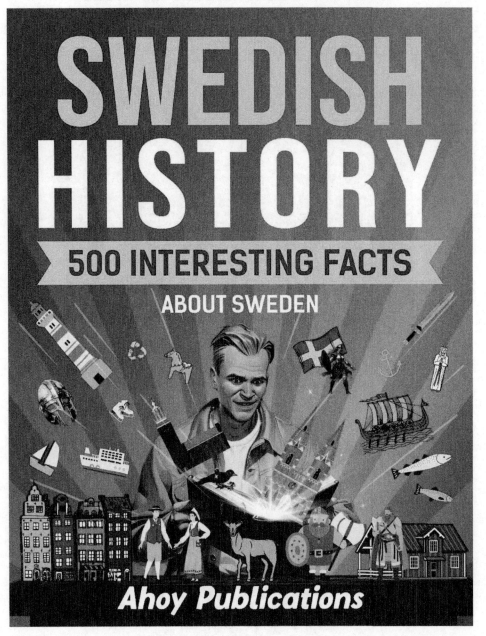

Sources and Additional References

"Prehistory and Ancient History." Denmark.dk, Denmark.dk, 20 Nov. 2020,

denmark.dk/en/culture-history/prehistory-ancient-history/.

Lysgaard, Martin. "The Ancient History of Denmark." Ancient History Encyclopedia,

Ancient History Encyclopedia, 27 Feb. 2013, www.ancient.eu/ Denmark/.

Abelsen, Ole. "Christianization: Conversion of Denmark to Christianity."

Encyclopedia Britannica, Encyclopedia Britannica, Inc., 15 Mar. 2019,

www.britannica.com/event/Christianization-conversion-of-Denmark-to-

Christianity#ref259445.

"Northern Seven Years' War." Encyclopedia Britannica. Encyclopedia Britannica, 8

June 2019, www.britannica.com/event/Northern-Seven-Years-War

"Danish Colonies Abroad." Christian V - Explorer of the Navy, Viking Maritime

Museum, vikingmaritimemuseum.com.au/christian-v-explorer-of-the-navy/

danish-colonies-abroad/.

Kyhl, Flemming. "The Great Northern War (1700-1721): The Battle of Copenhagen (1711)." Licensed Battlefield Guide Tom Emberland, Licensed Battlefield Guide, 30 Aug. 2020, www.licensedbattlefieldguide.com/great-northern-war-battles-1711-copenhagen/.

"Copenhagen 1711." Battlefields of Europe, Battles of the Great Northern War, 1711, The Battle of Copenhagen, 1711, www.battlefieldsofeurope.co.uk/1700-1721-great-northern-war/copenhagen-1711.

"The Monarchy & Constitution." The Monarchy & Constitution, www.denmark.dk/en/denmark/dorking-denmark/history/the-monarchy-constitution.

Davison, Mark. "The Making of a Nation: 1720-1750." Danish Roots – Genealogy and History of Denmark – Articles – Making of a Nation, danishroots.net/articles/the-making-of-a-nation-1720-1750/.

McClellan, William E. "Christian VII of Denmark." Encyclopedia Britannica, Encyclopedia Britannica, Inc., 15 Jan. 2020, www.britannica.com/biography/Christian-VII-king-of-Denmark.

"The Danish Enlightenment." Nordic academic press, www.nordicacademicpress.com/the-danish-enlightenment.

"The Kingdom of Denmark." Encyclopedia Britannica, Encyclopedia Britannica, Inc., 27 July 2020, www.britannica.com/place/Denmark/Government#ref19639.

Colket, Meredith, ed. The Age of Enlightenment: Studies in European History. Transaction Publishers, 2008.

Huerta, Robert. "Battle of Copenhagen (1801)." Encyclopedia Britannica, Encyclopedia Britannica, Inc., 11 Mar. 2019, www.britannica.com/event/Battle-of-Copenhagen-1801.

Li, Tiffany. "Napoleonic Wars - Impact, Causes & Definition of the Napoleonic Wars." History, A&E Television Networks, 20 Jan. 2021, www.history.com/topics/napoleonic-wars.

Pattullo, Polly. "The Loss of Norway: A Brief Overview." History on the Net, 3 Apr. 2013, www.historyonthenet.com/the-loss-of-norway-a-brief-overview/.

"Treaty of Kiel." Encyclopedia Britannica, Encyclopedia Britannica, Inc., www.britannica.com/topic/Treaty-of-Kiel.

Israel, Jonathan I., et al. Napoleon's War in Europe: The Conflict That Shaped a Continent. Palgrave Macmillan, 2014.

The Office of the Prime Minister, Denmark. "World War One." Denmark.dk, Denmark.dk, 13 Mar. 2019, www.denmark.dk/en/about-denmark/world-war-i/.

Hernon, Ian. "The Naval Battle of Jutland, 1916." Encyclopedia Britannica, Encyclopedia Britannica, Inc., 6 Aug. 2007, www.britannica.com/event/Battle-of-Jutland.

History.com Editors. "Nazi Germany Invades Denmark and Norway." History.com, A&E Television Networks, 5 Apr. 2010, www.history.com/this-day-in-history/nazi-germany-invades-denmark-and-norway.

"Nazi Germany Occupation of Denmark — Overview." World War II Guide, www.world-war-2.info/occupations/denmark/.

"The Danish Resistance." The Jewish Virtual Library, Jewish Virtual Library, Jewish Virtual Library, www.jewishvirtuallibrary.org/the-danish-resistance.

Kronquist, Jesper. "The Tourist Movements to, and from, Denmark." Danish Tourist Association, June 2012, www.turisme-danmark.dk/resources/The-Tourist-Movements-to-and-from-Denmark.pdf.

"Denmark Passes Renewable Energy Law." EU Climate Action, 20 June 2013, www.climate-action.org/denmark-passes-renewable-energy-law/.

Printed in Great Britain
by Amazon

56328739R10044